W9-AOU-671

DID A DINOSAUR DRINK THIS WATER?

Robert E. Wells

Albert Whitman & Company · Morton Grove, Illinois

For my sister Mary, who has been a lifelong supporter of my creative endeavors.

Library of Congress Cataloging-in-Publication Data

Wells, Robert E.
Did a dinosaur drink this water? / written and illustrated by Robert E. Wells.
p. cm.
ISBN 13: 978-0-8075-8839-0 (hardback)
ISBN 10: 0-8075-8839-3 (hardback)
ISBN 13: 978-0-8075-8840-6 (pbk.)
ISBN 10: 0-8075-8840-7(pbk.)
1. Water—Juvenile literature. I. Title.
GB662.3.W43 2006 551.48—dc22 2006001039

Text and illustrations copyright © 2006 by Robert E. Wells.
Published simultaneously in Canada by Fitzhenry & Whiteside, Markham, Ontario.
All rights reserved. No part of this book may be reproduced or transmitted in any form
or by any means, electronic or mechanical, including photocopying, recording, or by any
information storage and retrieval system, without permission in writing from the publisher.
Printed in the United States of America.
10 9 8 7 6 5 4 3 2

Hand-lettering by Robert E. Wells.
The illustration media are pen and acrylic.
Design by Carol Gildar.

Also by Robert E. Wells:
Can You Count to a Googol?
How Do You Know What Time It Is?
How Do You Lift a Lion?
Is a Blue Whale the Biggest Thing There Is?
What's Faster Than a Speeding Cheetah?
What's Older Than a Giant Tortoise?
What's Smaller Than a Pygmy Shrew?

Every living thing needs water. Without it, flowers and apple trees will never grow.

Fish live in water, ducks swim on top of water, and people need to drink it every day.

Water dissolves minerals and food substances, or NUTRIENTS, and carries them inside living things.

When you water an apple tree, the water dissolves minerals in the soil.

The water-mineral mix is absorbed by the roots

and drawn up through the tree trunk

to the leaves.

Then the leaves, using water, air, and the Sun's energy, produce nutrients for the apples.

Water comes in 3 forms: LIQUID, SOLID, and GAS.

When it's liquid, it pours. When it's solid, it's ice.

When it's heated, it EVAPORATES, changing into WATER VAPOR, an invisible gas.

On a warm day, there's nothing more refreshing than a glass of ice-cold water.

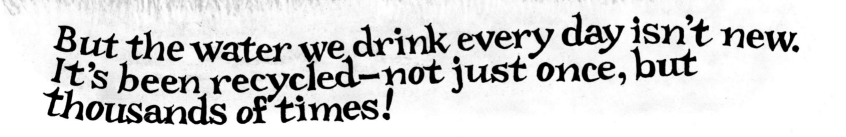

But the water we drink every day isn't new. It's been recycled—not just once, but thousands of times!

The water we drink today is made up of the same tiny particles, called MOLECULES, that have been on Earth for billions of years.

Some of those molecules may have been in a water hole that a dinosaur drank from 150 million years ago!

How can this be?

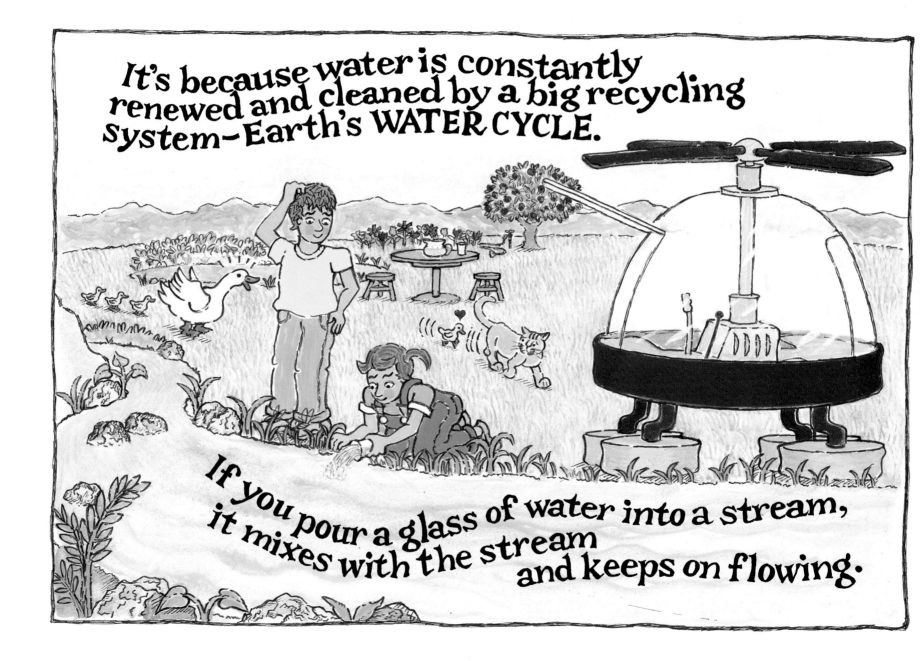

As the stream flows down the mountain, some of the impurities that are always in stream water are filtered out

as the water passes over and through rocks, pebbles, and plants.

Flowing streams are one of nature's ways of cleaning water as it moves through the water cycle.

into the ocean. Ocean water and river water are not the same. River water is FRESH WATER, and ocean water has lots of salt.

Even so, the waters mix and the river water becomes part of the ocean.

But that is not the end of the story.
Water doesn't *stay* in the ocean.

The sun heats the water on the surface of the ocean, and the water turns into its gas form: water vapor.

Aided by the wind, the water vapor rises in the air.

When it meets colder air, the vapor CONDENSES, or goes back to its liquid form.

It changes into billions of tiny water droplets we see as clouds.

The water in clouds is fresh, because as ocean water evaporates, it leaves the salt and other impurities behind.

Evaporation is one of nature's best water cleaners!

Now the wind blows some of the clouds over land,
and when the water droplets build up and grow heavier,

they fall as rain—or snow,
if the air is cold.

Some of the rain and snow falls right
back into streams, rivers, and the ocean—

but not *all* of it. At least, not for a while.

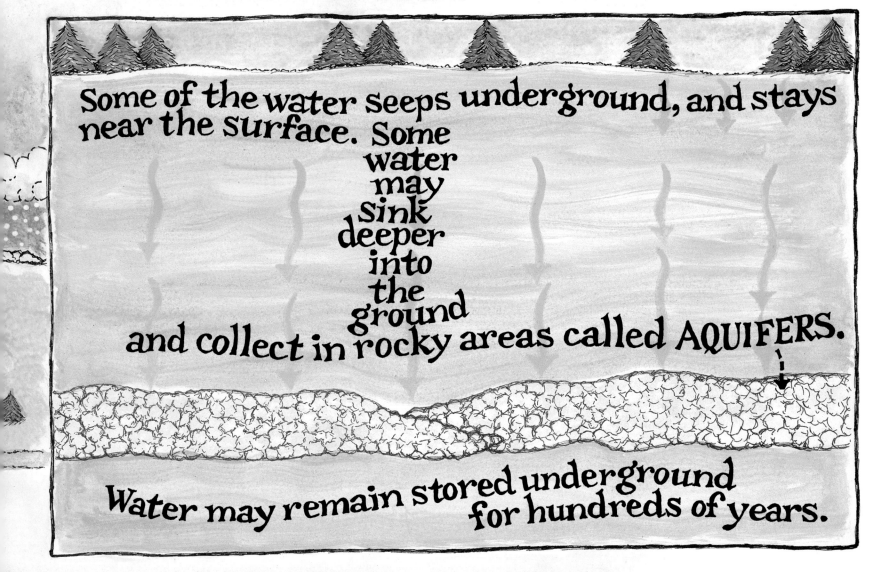

Some of the water seeps underground, and stays near the surface. Some water may sink deeper into the ground and collect in rocky areas called AQUIFERS.

Water may remain stored underground for hundreds of years.

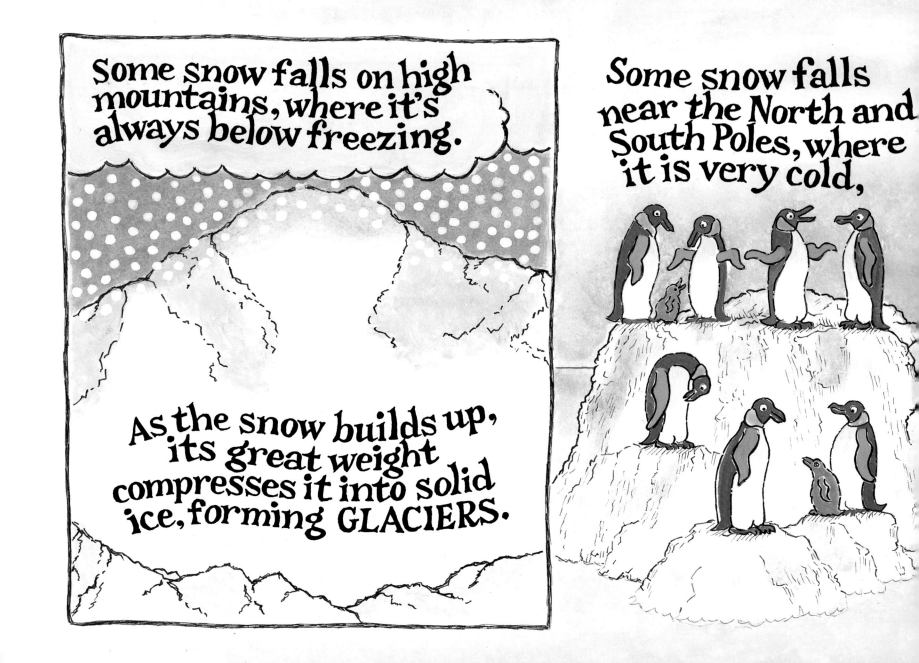

Some snow falls on high mountains, where it's always below freezing.

As the snow builds up, its great weight compresses it into solid ice, forming GLACIERS.

Some snow falls near the North and South Poles, where it is very cold, and becomes part of the polar ice. ICEBERGS are chunks of polar ice floating in the ocean.

Water may stay frozen in glaciers and polar ice for thousands of years.

Most of Earth's fresh water is frozen in polar ice and glaciers—or stored under the ground!

Eventually, most of the underground water seeps out into rivers, lakes, and the ocean. Polar ice and glaciers melt and become part of ocean water.

Ocean water evaporates, and the cycle repeats— over and over and over again.

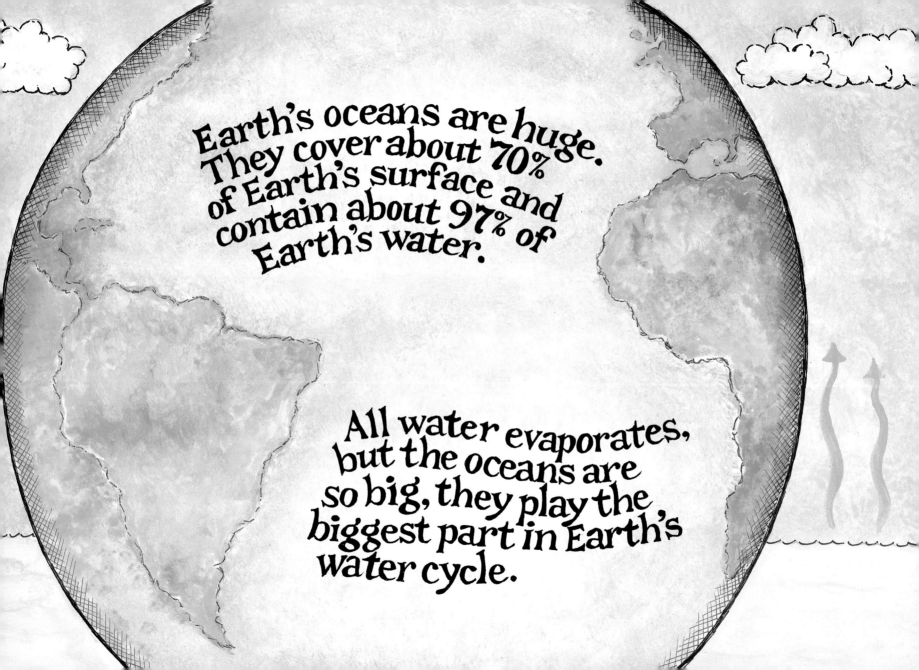

Earth's oceans are huge. They cover about 70% of Earth's surface and contain about 97% of Earth's water.

All water evaporates, but the oceans are so big, they play the biggest part in Earth's water cycle.

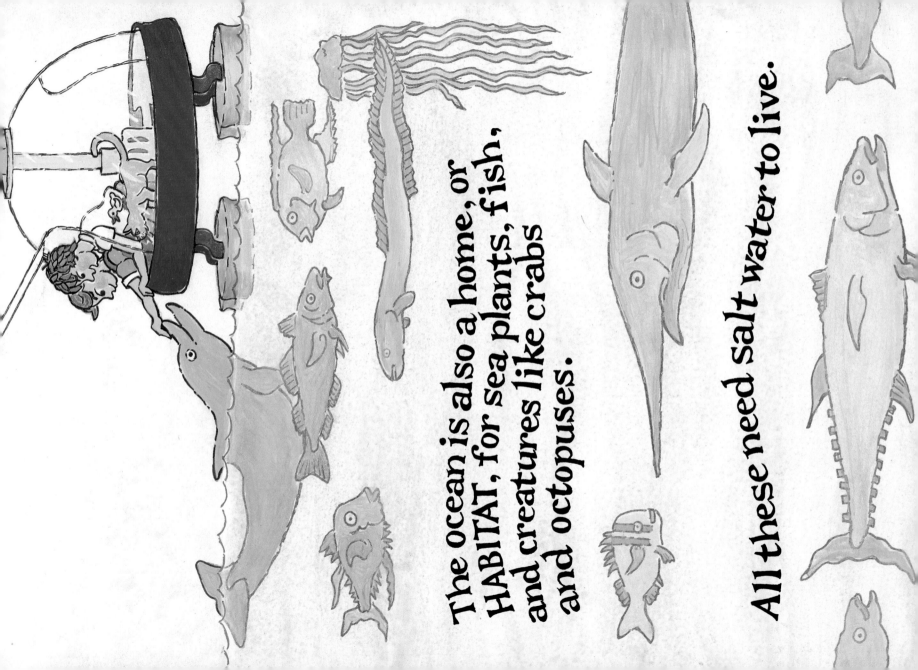

The ocean is also a home, or HABITAT, for sea plants, fish, and creatures like crabs and octopuses.

All these need salt water to live.

Millions of people depend on fish and other sea life for food every day.

Streams, rivers, and lakes are fresh water. They provide habitats for living things that need fresh water —

plants and trees, birds insects, and animals.

The fresh water in lakes and rivers is used by people for drinking, washing, cooking, and growing food.

We sail on it, swim in it, and fish in it.

Lake and river water can even make the lights in your house go on!

Some rivers have **DAMS**. A dam is a huge wall that controls the flow of the river. The water that is held back collects in a lake, or **RESERVOIR**, behind the dam.

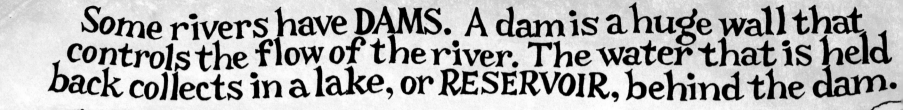

WELCOME
to
RIVERFLOW
DAM
"YOUR WATER AT WORK"

When the reservoir water is released and flows through the dam, it creates energy to make electricity.

Electricity made with flowing water is called HYDROELECTRICITY.

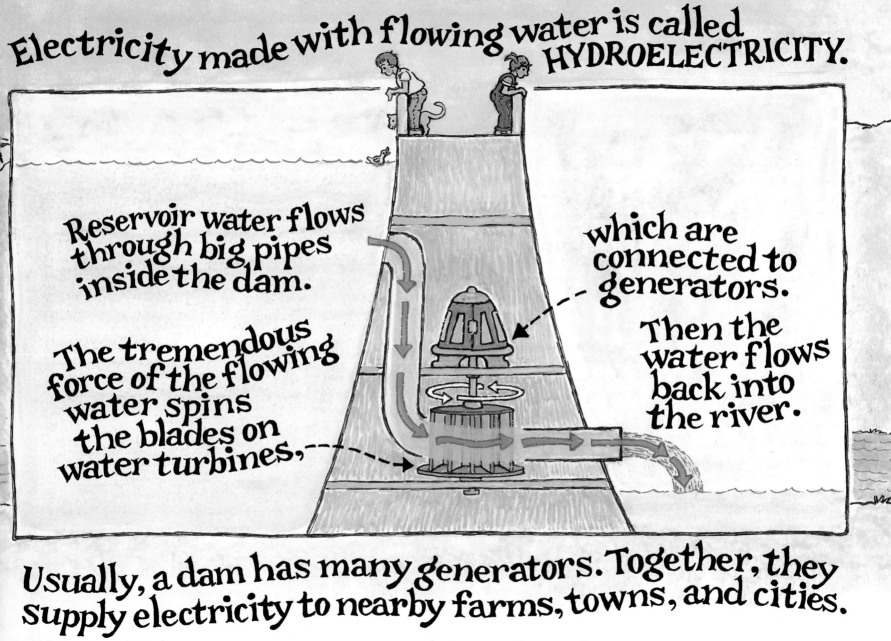

Reservoir water flows through big pipes inside the dam.

The tremendous force of the flowing water spins the blades on water turbines,

which are connected to generators.

Then the water flows back into the river.

Usually, a dam has many generators. Together, they supply electricity to nearby farms, towns, and cities.

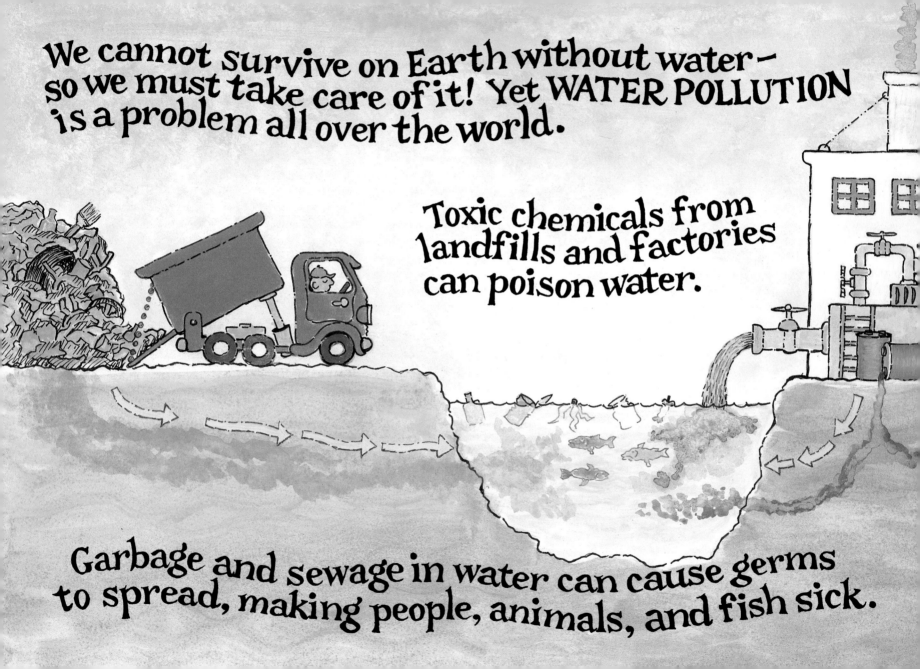

We cannot survive on Earth without water — so we must take care of it! Yet WATER POLLUTION is a problem all over the world.

Toxic chemicals from landfills and factories can poison water.

Garbage and sewage in water can cause germs to spread, making people, animals, and fish sick.

EARTH'S WATER AT WORK

Whether it's liquid, ice, or vapor, water goes about its work in many ways.

Sometimes water works as though it were an artist. Over millions of years, rivers, streams, and rain have helped, by erosion, to shape scenic mountain ranges. Glaciers have inched their way down mountains, carving magnificent valleys. And, because water expands with great force when it freezes, it has helped to create beautiful jagged cliffs and mountain peaks—by freezing and thawing in small rocky cracks and crevices, breaking rocks apart.

Steam is water vapor that comes from boiling water. Steam also expands with great force, just as ice does—and the power of steam has been put to use in many ways. In years past, people rode in steam-powered trains on land, navigated up and down rivers in steamboats, and crossed oceans in steamships. Today, steam-powered turbines generate much of the world's electricity.

And did you know that the oceans, along with all the other things they do, help make living on Earth more comfortable? It's because water is very good at storing the sun's heat. Ocean currents, moved by the wind, circulate sun-warmed water by the shores of every continent, helping to make climates more moderate on all the world's land.

Almost everywhere you go, you can see—or feel—the results of Earth's water at work!